Esperanza's Hair

Alabama Poetry Series

General Editors: Dara Wier and Thomas Rabbitt

PEGGY SHUMAKER

Esperanza's Hair

The University of Alabama Press

Library of Congress Cataloging in Publication Data

Shumaker, Peggy, 1952–
  Esperanza's hair.

  (Alabama poetry series)
  I. Title.   II. Series.
  PS3569.H778E8   1985   811'.54   84-16224
  ISBN 0-8173-0261-1
  ISBN 0-8173-0262-X (pbk.)

The epigraph to Section I is from *Labyrinths, Selected Stories & Other Writings* by Jorge Luis Borges, copyright © 1962, 1964 by New Directions Publishing Corporation. Used by permission.

The epigraph to Section II is from the title poem of *Things That Happen Where There Aren't Any People* by William Stafford. Copyright © 1980 by William Stafford. Reprinted with the permission of BOA Editions, Ltd.

A portion of the epigraph to Section III is from the third elegy in *The Duino Elegies* by Rainer Maria Rilke, translated by J. B. Leishman and Stephen Spender, copyright © 1939 by W. W. Norton & Company, Inc., copyright renewed 1967 by Stephen Spender and J. B. Leishman. Used by permission of W. W. Norton & Company, Inc. and The Hogarth Press.

The epigraph to Section IV is from *31 Letters and 13 Dreams* by Richard Hugo, copyright © 1977 by W. W. Norton & Company, Inc. Used by permission.

The epigraph to "A Crack in the Balanced Ship" is from *The Odyssey* by Homer, translated by Albert Cook, copyright © 1967 by Albert Cook. Used by permission.

In memory of Hanna Zoe Howe

In honor of Harriet L. Moen

ACKNOWLEDGMENTS

Many thanks to the editors and publishers of the journals in which these poems first appeared:

The Agni Review: "The Apple"
AWP Anniversary Awards 1982: "Esperanza's Hair"
Bits: "Mastectomy"
Calliope: "Cima Saddle," and in earlier versions "Desert Garden" and "The Raisin"
Cincinnati Poetry Review: "The Wife"
Graduate English Papers: "A Crack in the Balanced Ship"
The Greenfield Review: "Cutting the Storm"
Laundromat anthology: "Landlady," "A Crack in the Balanced Ship," "Chinese Print: No Translation"
The Louisville Review: "The Welldigger," "Getting Ready," "The Lever Between Her Breasts"
The Missouri Review: "Esperanza's Hair"
Mr. Cogito: "Baking"
Mountain Newsreal: "Mrs. Falbusch," "A Pure and Simple Easy Choice"
New Mexico Humanities Review: "Pancho Villa Meets El Mudo, the Deaf Shopkeeper"
Nimrod: "Ira and Amy Pratt," all sections
permafrost: "Canyon de Chelley: The Weaver," "A Few Chores," "A Man with a Stocking Cap"
Poets On: Regrets: "Jigsaw Puzzles"
Prickly Pear, Tucson: "Nellie Lopez"
Salome: "Wanting to Take the Dancer Home"
Things Bigger Than We Are anthology: "The Flight of the Moth"
Three Rivers Poetry Journal: "A Cotton Chopper Arches"
Writers Forum: "Landlady"

"Ladybugs" was first published in *Phantasm*, Vol. 4, No. 4 (copyright 1979, Heidelberg Graphics, Chico, CA).

Contents

III

IV

I

The leopard did not know, could not know, that he longed for love and cruelty and the hot pleasure of tearing things to pieces and the wind carrying the scent of a deer, but something suffocated and rebelled within him. . . .

—Jorge Luis Borges

Esperanza's Hair

Near the square in the dead part of town
the widow of the herbalist hums.
Still lovely, she tends him,
then scents her long hair.

She allowed the embalmer his ceremony,
but sent the bearers away.
The herbalist won't get out of his hammock.
He listens to her because her hands rub his feet.
He dreams of her hands, long and narrow
as a man's hands, bringing gunboats
of potatoes, spinach, shrimp
steaming to their table. He dreams of her hair
glued to her skin, after they use her body.

You sang, she says, wet my mouth,
numb my nose and skin.
We have this beginning. I remember
you brought me canned goods, plates.
But you told me wrong.

I tried to get away. I packed my combs,
but the raft wouldn't hold.
The river took charge of my articles.

The grape-colored water stirs
small hosannas. I do not deny that this gift
of denial is a real gift. But the heat-engines
in my body take special pains, like a sailor's letter.

3

So I wash my face under a corner lamp.
I twist my hair up for you. That's why.
I never thought there was a history to it.

A Crack in the Balanced Ship

> Since you wish to be on the balanced ship,
> I shall not push you off.
>
> —Telemachos

Bored with the perfect geometry of four legs,
four walls, all the right angles,
a young wife lives for the third part of the night
after stars balance heat and this raw-flesh age.

Thinking, she shakes the yoke:
marriage is salt, vital and basic;
mine, a salted mine
where promise catches light
but the miner comes home dirty.

Stroking the appalling softness below her belly
she splits into two sisters who can't stand to share
the same room. They agree to live on alternate days.

The river one, in love with casual water, sings,
What do you do with the other men
after you promise a husband?

The earth one, watching stars row past,
crafts a balanced ship
and does not give way.

Landlady

Her face is deep gray,
spider webs drooped over handfuls of dirt

Twilight settles like a dog on the porch
with my textbook Spanish, her toothless grin

Talk of her children and .the pain in her side
which returns each time they leave

News of the new grandson, healthy,
plans for a garden

Then her rough spotted hand
like a wing on my knee

proudly announcing *la boda bellisima*, her youngest
                                                    niece
and a handsome mechanic, *con mariachis, un baile, y*
                                    mucha comida

then quiet, as her eyes travel down
her legs, two wide loaves of french bread

poking out beneath her skirt
and she whispers,

    Mi hijita, don't marry. Leave yourself time.
    Learn this: I am ugly inside from waiting.

The Told Secret

A young woman tells a secret which she has promised
never to reveal. But slyly, so no one might accuse
her of telling, and no one can be sure it was she
who told. So now she has two secrets—the one
she has betrayed, and the fact of her treason.
Over the years, the weights of these intimacies
settle in her knees, which groan and creak and
remind her with a whole repertoire of pains the depths
of her duplicity. Because she cannot move, she gains
a reputation for stability. Troubled people
seek her out, people with unspeakable difficulties.
They confide in her relentlessly, each secret adding
its own specific weight to her body until even
her eyelids can no longer support themselves.
When she has absolutely room for no more, she hands
back an old confidence in exchange for each new one,
a trading of guilt across generations.
The old people's grievous embarrassments
the young take home as party favors.
Early on, this secret woman discovers that Truth in fact
is the greatest lie, so she always and immediately tells
what she sees. Everyone finds her insanely amusing.
In her later years she is much in demand
at dinner parties. One evening
a young woman does not laugh, though
everyone else in the room leans for balance
on the slim arms of potted palms. The old woman
draws the girl away, into the tiled kitchen.
Listen. I have something to tell you.

Bonifacia, the Violinist

When her fingers danced, she could afford
sweet peas and calendulas, the rain
of orange halos around their jar.

But now, when her mat airs in the cool
of the morning, Bonifacia, alone,
draws a horsehair bow over and back

across the seasons. Her lyrics expose
the stupidest of plants, banana and calabash,
that step to the tune any man plays.

Each evening men come, none very young,
and drop coins in the red saucer
Mauricio won

by floating a dime
just past the goldfish
just over the rim.

She calls to him,
Bring me a candle, presses her legs
against the only thing cool, her whitewashed wall.

Hugging her shadow,
she hears the military clink
of his lighter and turns her face.

Night passes without squeaking. He turns her
this way and that.
You choose, she says,

thinking of dishtowels
spangled with sunflowers
Mauricio chose to curtain their room.

He promised to send for them,
but the flowers faded, washed away.
Sour as an old washcloth, the butcher's breath

cools her neck. But she smells Mauricio
rich with sweat, his private music
rattling her bones.

His daughter brings home drawings now:
elaborate hats for all the people,
bonnets smothered in passion fruit and orchids

and round o's
on their bellies
but no clothes.

The Wife

He leaves her on the farm, where doors don't lock,
and takes the household pistol on his rounds.
She stands for twenty years across the field
and breathes his dust. At night he tries to stroke
her hair: she stiffens up. His hand lies cracked
behind his knee. Yet when the gin forecloses
his tab, or Tony's Chinese Market calls,
she soaks the beans like always, and understands
that loving him means knowing that her chance
to ripen whole is small. She wanders back
into the burnt and puny cotton, sags against
the palo verde's trunk. The branches
rattle, full of pods. Her boots leave streaks
in mud as she crams white bolls in gunny sacks.

Chinese Print: No Translation

Without warning, the woman says,
  Our marriage has become a business.
How can you say that, when you know I love you, etc. etc.,
  her husband cries. He serves her pirouettes and Earl Grey
  on porcelain dishes, but it's not enough.
What can I give you? What do you want?
  But secretly, so far I'm the only man brave enough
  to take you on, and you know it. Still,
What can I give you? What do you want?
  But if he has to ask, it doesn't count.
As in, if he can't swim naked at midnight
  on a deserted beach
  without worrying about phosphorescent plankton
  and our traveler's checks, forget it.
At dawn, she washes up on the beach,
  fire-coral dreams searing her thighs.
Brown UPS trucks search for her husband, each one
  delivering what has to be signed for.

Why It Startles Him, That Way She Slices Pineapple

The next morning he hears it all,
her breadboard drawn out from under the sink,
the sucking closure
of the round-shouldered fridge.
Without seeing, he knows. Pineapple.

One clean stroke severs the head,
two more halve and quarter. Quick hollowing,
and she sets four armored boats rocking in the sea
of sweet water draining from their own flesh.
Her lips only
smile.

Last night as he stumbled awake
needing suddenly to fasten the latch
on the screen that leads to the porch,

her face sailed past, a ship of light
voyaging beyond him, her dreams stowed away.

Packing off for a new life,
a caravan of spices, she's *la conquistadora*,
mapping out the places the moon can't reach.

What anchor can he offer?
What port? His world,
where bees have no sting
and no honey? No.

Her view of the universe, his too, vaults through
instruments made by her own hands,

like these not-quite triangles of pineapple
refusing to come to the point.

It could be a gesture of tenderness,
her offering of fruit.
Neither of her hands understands
why he draws his breath in, fast,
why he casts down his eyes, lost
in the pain of her leaving.

It's early yet.
Light snags on the juice
dripping down her wrist. Her tongue
lifts one drop from the blue highways.
Her tongue follows.

With a Man I Wasn't Married To

It was only for a moment
in a town I didn't live in
with a man I wasn't married to
and a car I didn't own.
The young man frying onions
in his hidden kitchen
behind the counter of the pension
recommended this little place
on Washington Square.
They make their own noodles.

Cafeteria racks of fresh pasta
dry in measured heaps, tangled
neatly. The barkeep handles
the raw steaming swoosh
of the cappuccino machine
like some ship's captain,
sure and direct.
Fettucini al Basta—
a religious experience—
herbs and butter,
fragrant, tender,
pasta al dente,
one moment complete.

Sure, our rent-a-Mustang
double-parked in the tow-away zone
is just asking for it. I know
that blond waiter
working this summer job
keeps track of everything
in his long black book.
Of course, we'll pay.
But not yet.
Bracing for the fog-wind
whipping through the spires,
lights splash on
across the bay.
Meters tick. Every minute
lovers' talk charges the wires.
Through the mist, lights pierce
their small holes, half-remembered
scenes from blurry-edged dreams.

It was only for a moment
and I was far away and ready.
I can't speak for everyone.
But I know in my shyness
that I can endure
small doses of heaven.

Detroit in April

Forty floors up, remember?
way past the reach of ladders of firemen,
I come to your room
in the shimmering cylinder hotel.
Across the river is a foreign land
where they take better care of the trees.
Over here it's motor city, cruising.
Detroit: red neon—a bald sign uptown
shrieking *Medusa Cement*.
We both see the snakes, but neither one
freezes. Instead of stone,
soft laughter like moving water.
We watch coins
turning on the surface
every place the river shifts.
Clothes fall away
without our help almost.
Listen. The wind is not talking
to us. We make instead its noises,
aching with possibility, young
for a while. Now. April.
You take me apart real fast
and stir me up
till my heart churns
like a horse
that's blind and running.

The office workers
corralled across the way—
there they are! We wave,
and know by their quick turning
they have seen.
Shining on the inside
better than the building and the river and the lights,
we're wide open as April,
forty floors out of reach.
Such witnesses could swear
we know each other. Will they
nudge each other and grin,
glad for our thrashing?
Or maybe throw—what? we wonder—
in the river on the way home tonight.

Mastectomy

Two river toads hunch

in a stainless-steel pan and it's over.

Instead of breasts, slices of raw liver

and a cavity no husband's tooth can fill.

Her bras hang, empty feedbags folded back,

as she trims the ivy.

She finds a black widow clutching her egg sacs,

huge gossamer teardrops, like breasts.

I understand, she wheezes as she crushes the widow.

Forgive me, I understand.

II

And out there in the country a rock has been
waiting to be mentioned for thousands of years.
                                        —William Stafford

Jesse James Jim Draws a Picture of Home

Just the head
of the horse shows,
nipping past the east side of the hogan
to catch in its yellowed teeth
fraying cuffs of the cowboy shirts
flapping on the line.

The man on his way to the outhouse
works loose the buttons of his fly.
No one is there
to have to turn away.

Past all fences
the mesa rides,
low and wide.

Waves of sheep tatter by
under the hissing stick of a sister
saying *tsxį́į́ł, tsxį́į́ł,* hurry, sheep.

All the empty parentheses,
hoofprints, their code never broken.
Hoofprints vanishing
over rock. Broken loose, this land,
poured free from earthen vessels.

So hard, running,
out of breath, kids
chasing a wagon
winding down the lane.
So hard, feet quick
whipping and stirring a thick
red wake.

Smoke clears over the blue crater
where the boarding school used to be.

The sharp green flecks
Jess does not explain.
Bits of Thunderbird
shattered and left
to glitter like some foreign saint's eyes,
evil in red earth.

Canyon de Chelley: The Weaver

Corn straggles dry
below me: the weaver
who measures with two fingers
the colors in a pattern
to keep luck in.
One thread leaves a way out,
a hole in the fence, like the one
Miréy chased the sheep through before I could shut up
her barking. We whacked the lambs,
played keep away
with the missionaries.
We smelled of wood smoke
chased round and round
in a round stove, a round house.
My daughter, too, smells of wood smoke,
rich, as she ought to.
She'll make pottery, black like Maria's.
By the river of oranges,
she'll hunt polishing stones.
Traders will come
to wait for her, watching
our burros in rope neckties
shave circles in wild grass.
Yes, traders will come
to wait for her to name a price,
and they will say please.

Blue Corn, Black Mesa

Before you go, I need to tell you
why here tongues turn dry as piki bread.
No one knows why this story is true

but I know there was a woman who
buried both hands in blue dough. She said,
Before you go, I need to tell you

why Hopi corn grows short, in a few
spindly clumps, not deep and wide and red.
No one knows why this story is true,

but I know it is not a lie. New
seed lay still; the sheep we gave for dead.
Before you go I need to tell you

that crater's spirit gave us breath. Blue
winds swept ash from the mesa, it bled—
no one knows why this story is true—

earth's sky blood washed ragged furrows. Blue
corn cracked, tucked sharp in this lava bed.
Before you go, I need to tell you:
no one knows why this story is true.

Note: Hopi blue corn is a biological riddle. It germinates only in
   thin volcanic soil and thrives in the severe, unforgiving climate of
   the high desert.

Cutting the Storm

Thunderstorms stomped Viejita Lujan's garden,
so Mamá made sure about ours.
She sent me, hurry up, down the street
to borrow the neighborhood's other silver knife
while she double-checked what you do.
La Cuentista said:

>She who faces the storm
>must be married in the church
>and to prove it
>wear forever on her finger
>a band of silver or of gold.
>Two silver knives
>(we had one) she must cross
>over her head after the sun
>has abandoned us.
>With her face to the West,
>she must spread her feet
>wide as her shoulders
>and begin to sharpen
>against one another
>the unholy blades.
>The storm will rest
>directly over her head
>¡ahorita! that's the time—
>cut it quick
>into more pieces
>than machaca,
>pieces its mother

could not recognize.
Then gather every member
who eats food from your table
and say with one mouth
thank you,
we are sure now—
this is not the year we will starve.

Pancho Villa Meets El Mudo, the Deaf Shopkeeper

Cananea, Mexico, 1910

Guns first, then beans,
and when the bin held only dust,
threats with the shoulder-fitted parts
of smuggled rifles.
In a good year, my father,
El Mudo, haggled in sign language
three pesos, take it or leave it
over a kilo of pintos heaped in their freckles
on the wide steel scoop.
But that year the only pods we split
grew high up, out of reach—
palo verde and mesquite,
frijoles indios. Our bellies
rose just a little that year,
tight round pouches of not enough.
Mother was glad she could not hear
the empty languages of stomachs.
God, she was lovely, even with
four kids and a dog.
When the raiders glanced around
for a ripe girl, they weren't sure
if her defect should protect her.
Then they saw my father
pushing under their mustaches
prize saddles, unstained bridles.
My hearing brother remembers they yelled

words he couldn't know, but he knew
were bad, so Dad threatened them
with the mysterious omniscience
of silence. He simply stood,
lifted his chest, and clenched
one fist at a time.
His long nightshirt split the black air
and they saw him there, part specter,
part saint, a still white smear
blasting their plans.
So they painted us a few nightmares—
tore into our mattresses,
broke all the plates. Ripped even
the one down comforter
kept for decoration on the bedstead
beside the baby's crate, and the baby
moved his mouth like a fish-mouth
calling the white riot *beautiful*,
he didn't know any better. To him,
this was a game, spinning feathers
with his breath.
Yucca pointed the way, scattered
Villa's men, they
showed their knifeblades
to my father, then swung right legs
over their horses.
David said it lasted long after
we couldn't see. Those horses' feet
made the sounds of hell, he said,
but I wouldn't know. All that time
my own feet cramped around the sack
my father had stuffed up under my hem.
America was in that sack,
I just didn't know it then.

Nellie Lopez

Please accept this spiral of beargrass
    lashed tight with yucca
split into wheatstitch.
    Nellie Lopez made it herself,

soaking the dry weeds
    she gathers from silent places
near the devil's claw.
    Right by the cross

where Rosario drowned,
    I found her, straightlegged
in the sand, her ankles crossed
    in the Papago way.

She said that the river
    told her to expect me
though the Gila runs now
    only in hard times

when brown walls of water
    foam over whole villages
and Nellie has to dig out
    and start over.

She asked who would use this circle
    woven in times of little rain.
I told her what I know of you:
    that you listen

to the whispers of your own heart
   even when the world shouts;
that rice and beans nourish you less
   than the music you carry.

I told her you never slept outside
   a night in your life
that you didn't hear that dry rattle
   when the bank caves in

earth gasping, dust smothering
   you frozen
right there, blind
   where your heart stopped.

Then broken smiles and broken breath
   while the snake clears out
leaving you hacking in the throat,
   shaky, so glad for the stars.

Free Sample

The pale baby on the label
smiles in another language.
Nurses volunteer formula talk,
mixing and boiling, to ripped, sedate mothers.
Their sharp teats hurt with tight milk,
ripen round two new thumbs of nipple.
Refused the suck, they shrink back or sag
or maybe perk up. Refused suck, the baby's lips
wither on powder slicked too much
with public water.

Mother pounds her belly flat again
again flat before the moon burns
so no one will see
that she might get old.
Until one day the powder is gone
and the baby isn't
and white halls glare
emergency. Emergency. The hollow steel
in his temple vein traveling sugar.
First son, *hijo*, cheeks stretching
barely over his skull.

She waits.
Picks a scab, feeling far away
each bit break loose. Death
wells out, not hers,
and she eats it.

A Cotton Chopper Arches

Snorting pumps spew the only water running for miles
down fuzzy chutes whose millipede legs feed
cotton, milo, sugar beets. Lunchtime choppers
dangle on the bank, laugh at the fossil finish
left from frogs in the hopper when the ditch was poured.
Kids toss illegal rocks, duck in themselves.

The rows radiate waves of blue heat,
washing ankles, stems, roots. Dry as jerky,
a woman chopper minds her business,
her arms separate from her body
her automatic body separate from her self.

Each stone her boy throws in the ditch
is a piece of her: an ear, a hand,
a backbone handful. It hurts most, finally,
that backbone handful, so she hacks
harder at the furrow's spine
till the heels of her hands shove her pelvis forward.

Steaming in a Cattle Tank Filled by Medical Springs

Eight Irish whiskeys, but just two Irishmen,
plenty enough company for wives to get lost.
Soaking loose the foaming low groans
of cattle, soaking out a hard day's mended fence,
one confesses, "I have always wanted your wife."
The other, "I had yours."
One lies.
Stars wheel and lock;
the whole night slams on its brakes.

The glass door slides clearly open.
Both damp women
wrap their hair in peach-colored
question marks, their temples
blue under false light.

Simple cruelty, romance kept alive,
held in
by four hands, sprawling,
roots of the thorn, the sage.

Cima Saddle

The patch snow thickens
in the shade, hiding the trail
on purpose.

We keep our way
by the distant splinter
of a frozen waterfall.

At Cima Saddle
we shelter in time,
cook, and watch the night eating.

Squatting in the moist ring
scraped around the firepit,
we try the green nuts.

Praying for Scars

Along the Mogollon Rim
from Young to Payson
toppers lop the tips off ponderosa pine,
clearing the high-wired air.

Boots with teeth bite hard,
barking up a foothold.

Laid back tight in his
wide leather sling,
the new guy jerks twice,
pulleyed tense for his saw.

She rises to him, smiling,
chained partner still willing to flirt.
So high, pure air seduces.

The topper steadies his hips
and balances pressure, flak,
the tree's resistance. Half through,
the chain snags a fist of rock
knotted deep in the grain,
a stone lifted from under the earth
and levitated over the innocent years
of his coming up, agate shoved up
as the sap rose each sticky season.

They were both out of place in the air.

The steel teeth spit, and the saw
bucked, a twister-arching bronc
cracking branches backwards,
splitting him that quick
axehead hard on a firm wedge,
split him clean as a seasoned rail.
Arm alone, cheap flap
of tissue and bone, first-aid bandana
limp. No better kiss to make it better.
The foreman tied him sitting up,
roped the loose arm fast
to his chilling side.
The ground was red before he got there.
Christmas trees lay slaughtered all around.
From every mouth, prayers for scars,
for something to show when he might tell this story,
prayers for the angry breath of proud flesh.

III

Look, we don't love like flowers, with only a single
season behind us; sap older than memory
rises in our arms when we love.

—Rainer Maria Rilke

Ira and Amy Pratt

1. Ira Pratt, Standing in Sawdust

He wanted the scraps, so Ira Pratt agreed
That Morrison's old rosewood piano could
Under his steady hand reawaken
As a fine, long desk with every joint fitted
Smooth as the fingerbends of the hedgehog
Wedged last summer under the porch,
Visiting for the first time on this house
The rancid-butter odor
Of a death too slow in coming.

                                     It swept up
Into Amy's tufted horsehair parlor,
Into her hushed taffeta sleeves, frightening
In their demeanor, as if some terrible beast
Just made it, crawling, up to her elbow
And exploded there,
Raining its uncompromising black juices
Over stiff tucks and stays all the way down,
Missing only her collar, sparingly tatted
In the spiral tendency of morning glories,
The white fibers irritable and delicately poised,
A collar of the sort worn only
By victims of their own pursuits,
By women talking with shaking fingers
About a man who could lift out the very soul
Of a fine instrument and lay it aside,
Making room for a secret drawer where men could hide

The fine-grained poems of winters spent
Looking forward to the season when men
Would be sent away, when even boys
Who knew the names of all the constellations
Could not be permitted behind the house
Where women gathered twice a year
To unanchor themselves the great square mouth
Of the cistern and draw up fresh cedar buckets
Brimming with water soft as long petticoats
Unstarched for summer.

2. *Ira Pratt, Preparing for the Day*

This washing of the hair
Was something one got ready for,
A ceremony demanding help
And a strict division of labor.
Ira knew it was his place
To dance hard of an evening
His intricate dance of letting go,
A hard dance for a man without liquor,
Doubly hard for Ira,
A spurious dance unfitting a sober believer in romance.
Without even whiskey's redemptive excuse,
Ira's raspy bones invited some fatal courage
To open two buttons on the bodice of Amy's good silk,
Forcing him then to blink
Her barn-dust and wool-grease scowl
Out of his eyes, making him admit
That the glint of moonlight on her hair
Reminded him of scrap metal,
Clanking all the way home.

Raingutters he put up with his own hands
Caught the water heating now
Over unscuttled coal and the kindling Amy split herself
And stacked during those mannerly weeks
Ushered into their house in unclouded anticipation
Of this day of the unleashing of ankle-length hair.

On a day of towels softened and folded nearby,
Of dawn-hour basins hauled to the bench,
Amy's arrangement of washing soda and extract of pine
Promised to return to her
The untamed aroma of the forest she was
Before Ira gave her children,
Especially this little one
Who squirmed in to impose even on her name,
Amy, after her, taking her name before she was done
                                        with it,
A young woman in a dress turned only once,
With years yet before she need worry
About what reaches up out of the cushions
Of a horsehair sofa
To pull perfectly good and indignant people
Down on their backs and pin them there.

3. *Ira Pratt, Welcoming Venus to North Dakota*

                                        Afterthought.

No one mumbled this word
So true of the new child,
The Amy everyone knew
By her plumskin voice,
This cream-singing

Runt of the litter
Whom Ira himself cuddled close
When the women ignored her away,
Chased her with their backs
Turned in the bed of day lilies
Recently sprung from misplaced bulbs,
Ira's lilies,
Sodden under wrist-thick coils
Twisted with borrowed hands.
Without wringing,
The hair might sour,
So each twist climbed closer
To one mortal scalp,
Each woman clenching
As if to release
From her expectant flesh
A better self, some whole woman,
Just born, but looking already
Very much like someone else,
Startled in her ephemeral underwear.
Dry places lightened on the ground.
Twice a year the women risked
This chance to be cleaner,
More desirable,
Untried in the way
That cancels out children.
Disguised by their nakedness,
The women had no hands left
To take her in, so Amy ran,
Longing only to be older
And among them, to unwind her hair,
Knotted and elaborately bit
By hundreds of tortoiseshell teeth,

Grown hair as long as her life,
Longing to suffer longing as women do:
Purely, without object, without end.

But she was young, and could be comforted.
So her feet ran over turned ground
To Ira's woodshop, where the plane's metal tongue
Shoved away and away
Licked up a roomful of curls of her own
So she would not be jealous any more
Of the women unraveling
Three parts of their lives behind the house,
Lives holding still
The tight shapes they were bound to,
Freed only when wet,
Those lilies nodding
In wild daylight
Chilled through under rainwater
Saved for the shining rinse.

A handful of ringlets that would never relax
Ira fastened around his last child's face.
Watched her shake her head *no* to test
Wood's clean scrapings against her shoulders.
He hand-rubbed the finish on the neighbor's desk,
Then used the leftovers to fashion the narrow box
Balanced now on the little shelf of this new Amy's lap.
Ira watched her eyes dig into its corners,
Heard her voice tumble like loose beads.
She filled the box with music. Her song,
The song we all outgrow, Ira heard
Because he was not yet deaf,
That song a child must sing and a man must dance to,
Even in a shaded parlor, even in a box of his own.

43

The Welldigger

A flame darts from his thumbnail, balances
on the matchhead. *"Fyrstikker,"* he says.
"Folks don't think about fire anymore."

Lungs blazing with ice, they dig wells by hand.
He shovels dirt into the pail, hollers for Erling
to draw it up. Snorts once, hard, like a horse,
spits gritty mucus.

Five body-lengths down he squints up
at the creaking, his hand against the glare.
Erling kicks a frozen spike of earth off the edge.
Below, the pick takes one step before it falls.

Erling calls, "Engebretson? Hey?" and Hanna comes
                                                     out,
coarse flour powdering her hands like dirt.
Erl struggles him out of the hole. His hand is clamped
                                          over the wound
and puddles form in the hollows of his collarbones.

His stiff felt hat covers that dent
the rest of his life. But his children see
the fire, the wick of his body.

Ladybugs

Quarts of ladybugs
scraped off the grapevines
stir and moil in mayonnaise jars.
Here's luck crawling all over itself.

We watch the red and black
kaleidoscope until
Grandpa's shoes scrape on the porch
and the screendoor slams.

He squats down
to wirebrush our cheeks,
hums a hum Norwegian.
Still crusted with dirt,
his shoes boom like monster potatoes.

His shoes make things right:
when Lawrence and Welk staggered
and their whiskers lay still in the shoebox,
those shoes walked them out
under the walnut trees
and kicked the shovel into the ground.

But this time they stride
like church shoes
while he shakes the jars
and takes them outside.

We hear the lids unscrew
and the wings whisper.
He mumbles a few words
and they rise in unison,
a small tornado, that quart of spirit.

The Flight of the Moth

As they have no investment
  in any of this,
the peaks stand
  as they always have.

Now, in their shadow,
  a great moth
dries her wings,
  powdered with mica.

Her flight carries, slow, graceful,
  sheer weight of a prayer
offered for a promise
  two thousand years old.

Piñon-tight faces,
  cinder-stiff knees.
We take a side road
  marked by a row of broken stone.

The bike's teutonic murmur dies.
  Too many stars
and the yip and gitcha—
  coyotes in juniper.

Snap dry limbs open a little hole
  in the darkness, a red jewel
for the ear.
  All the trash

that goes with being human
    falls away. Fingers shimmer
like mica . . . and the heart curves
    upward, upward.

Heading to Show Low

It's dangerous
following the Superstitions
all the way to the end.
More than one prospector
died a legend
lost in those sharp canyons.
Rounding the bend,
an almost full moon
hovers like a host
held high
by a priest
robed in Lenten twilight.
Queen Creek tunnel yawns,
baring her just-brushed teeth,
promising the mysteries of a river of salt.
Just before I drive in
for one moment only
the cliffs flash with no pale fire,
no flame of small passion. No.
The hills leap up
out of their everyday clothes—
naked and red
they dance, they stretch, they offer
themselves one last time
to the sun.
I whip around
to catch the hills
furious in their passion,
to stretch wide and shout
Take me. Yes. Take me too.

But the patient moon
claims its own time.
Almost full, it climbs
past the black waterfalls
of Apache tears
blinding one prospector
at a time.

A Pure and Simple Easy Choice

In a dark room the size of a pigpen
my cousin and I hide from the babysitter.
I hold his hand flat against my chest.
I can hear us. Try me. All right.

Him, milking with one hand, groaning.
He just stands there, missing
from his movements. Nothing's inside
either. Point it where I tell you.

I hear my father. He comes in brisk and chipper,
tells us to stay in bed. My cousin has an argument
with himself. A little too pink,
that ring from his elastic. Take off

your whole pants. A pure and simple easy choice.
He starts hollering about that train to Memphis,
hot biscuits, look out now,
three kinds of preserves. Everything he's got

could be sold in one lump.
Keep still. I'll get it in . . .
Jesus!
he dies like an army cot.

Even Methodists

Before sun, that slow orange itch, itching already.
Outside, bougainvillea loaded with bees.
Heavy buzzing, not theirs, but the wooden
churning of a dasher
slapping my woman stomach inside.
Grinding urge, the chaos of ice cream.
Rocksalt and ice, hours of grinding,
rocksalt and ice, for three quick bites.
Boysenberries, peaches and cream.
All the slippery dashers, turning.

Beside me, sleeping hard, lies a man
with a heart wide open as a flatbed truck.
A man whose dreams I've carried so long
he thinks they are our children.
He would forgive me. Anything.
But he can't figure out itching
grown past friendly scratching,
can't break into the buzzing,
my beehives of loneliness.

It's M.Y.F. all over.
Fourteen and hurt bad,
I'm cowering hot in the arroyo
behind the dry A-frame of St. Paul's.
Inside, twenty-five freezers thicken
one quart at a time.
Today the multipurpose room
is no sanctuary. Delores yelled,
and she's my best friend,
Dirty-minded makeout
because I like it,
press my fingers into my body,
pray they are someone soon else's
wanting now me. Not allowed.
Not for Methodists. Right
then I knew hell. Still I'm knowing.
They forget.
We all come from lovers. All of us
buzz and itch and buzz.

Wanting to Take the Dancer Home

The sadness there is no reason for
invites herself in while the man is talking.
He's trying to make a point, a rather
important distinction. On the brink
of discovery, he pauses
to let his slower disciples catch up.

She begins to dance.
Her hands jangle like tambourines,
her legs ruffle and swirl. Everyone plans
to take her home, to wash her maroon breasts,
her cinnamon thighs. And when her dark lashes
seal the pact with you with you with you
with me, she swings away
on a blue vine, leaving behind
her scent: wet alfalfa, cut.

Watercolors

It's a juried show, this life,
forty pictures
hung against flat yellow walls,
one black telephone
waiting to ring.

Then it begins, the forgetting.
With a short walk into a familiar room
you arrive, but can't put your hand
on a reason. You thumb through
a novel from Peru, jumble a few drawers,
& hope in the search to unclutter
exactly what you're after.

Then someone you love takes off
for Tucson or Spain
or into a language so tender
you cry, wanting to follow.
Five minutes after she's gone,
she's silt
blurring on the bottom
of a tail-water pond.

Gone, the groomed slope
    of her cheekbone, gone
the sharp cliff
    of her left hip.
Even the parts you love best
    wash away.

Mysteries fade into secondhand denim.
Beside a row of twice-picked cotton
an amateur breaks out a fresh set
of brushes. Swishes stranded pigment
in a blue cracked mug.
Her rinsewater subdues
defined outlines, muddies
the pure landscapes
you really did see, visions
stacked against an off-white backdrop,
some framed, some ready to be crated.

Getting a Child

Sprawled over the hard Durham
the Northern Lights stuck together,
ribbons of dusty hard candy
swept up from under a straight-backed chair.
Three brothers filled the loft with new hay,
milked early, and wrapped their instruments
in freshly laundered flour sacks.
The Moentones, they called themselves,
set up under crimp-paper shades.

     Bradley's barn reeled!
Olga and Emma Broderick sashayed in
in costumes nobody'd ever seen
outside the wishbook. Promptly got sent,
wagging their bloomered tails
at the closed pastor's door, home.

A little past midnight
the fiddler's hand cramped.
He wobbled it, shook it hard,
flailed it as if flicking off
bedbugs dropped from some
infested upper bunk. Wouldn't loosen.
Guess that's it, Uncle Nels said,
and the married people set out.
Aunt Vieve sat in back. Had enough
of Nels, with his teeth in his mouth
and his bare elbows hanging out.

Right in front of God and everybody
Jamie Bradley planted a little peck
on Kathy Hansen's neck. She made the sound
of a scalded billy goat. Jamie tripped
his whole face bloodshot over that sound
all the way to his rig, running,
the big boys' gauntlet ready, yelling,
"Red goat, red goat, red goat, Bradley!"

The fiddler took the hand
of the legislator's graceful second daughter,
walked her around behind the cream station
where new rails stretched out light and clean
as pulled taffy. They were something,
those rails, rising above the dirt
people felt every day between their back teeth,
the dirt they breathed, draying up rocks
after harvest, scraping stoneboats
around the slough. The dust was so thick,
her foot fit exactly twice in his. He tucked his palm
in the untried scoop of her back,
took up his place natural as cotton plowline,
never expecting at this time of night
with a girl certainly who knew better
the Ex-press! flashing over ties and cinders,
the polished rails of his parallel ribs.
The engine of her spine built its momentum
pulling them both into smoke-swaying breaths,
gathering, gathering gathering steam . . .

No whistle blew.
But after a time, they knew—their skin
blushed in the northerly quality of the lights
folding and folding over themselves.
In this dirt, life was never a question
of pleasure, that licked and twisted thread
drawn clean through the needle.
They took the back way, simply,
her slippers too shallow,
the dust too deep. *Whatever this is,*
we are part of it.
They left each other wet.

IV

You watch them search your luggage. Then
you remember what you carry and start to explain.
                                    —Richard Hugo

By the Dunes at Yuma

As our rosy Studebaker bottomed out,
we bit the heads off turtles we'd just bought
and pulled away from the Wisteria Candy Cottage.
Miles before the dunes at Yuma
every branch and sandscoured plank
conjured grit-shocked stagecoaches
grinding along the old Butterfield line.
Mother dreamt of the subtle shifting
each fresh snip of wind cut loose.
My father never slowed. Except one time
when a thick wind head-on from Gila Bend
sandblasted eyebrows over both headlights.
We felt our way half-blind to the rest stop.
Land turned liquid, swelling, breaking.
In the bathroom, a swollen man
roading a blade clear back to Deming
kept warm all night
punching the hand dryer. The nozzle
bowed its head. My mom said,
"Look, you kids," and turned us
to face the storm we'd just come through:
Biggest living thing I've ever seen,
churning and cleansing,
tumbling gouged stones down from Jacumba.
Carving its own path, oblivious,
quickening in us
our own gritty history.

L'il Abner's

Before they fixed the place up
ropers used to heel each other and
jerk into loose dirt the drunkest
s.o.b.'s in from the ranch.
Naked women never had a chance—
the management tried to keep them,
genuine velvet, over the bar, but one
at least had always to hang
here by the door, so guys could rub her
and get lucky. My dad never roped
nor rode, nor put down boilermakers
till he couldn't see. Heck,
he just sold Chevies.
But he took us all in
on the way to the races,
Tucson Speedway, that halo of hay bales
where stock cars and micro midgets
bar-roomed in our ears
long past the checkered flag.
Yeah, he acted like Hank Arnold #1
who kissed the trophy girls always
whether or not he won. He took us in
like Abner's was a union meeting
and his dues all paid up, took us
and ordered three Cokes with two
cherries each and one Coors draft,
leaned over to elbow the raw jokes
that sent us girls by ourselves

to the john, where it clanged cowbells
and ripped sirens outside
whenever a woman sat down.

Jigsaw Puzzles

Just inside the kitchen door
of the house on Calle Ileo
the old Maytag twisted against her hoses
like a half-broken mare.
We were kids then. We never paid much attention.
The red dish drainer,
cruddy from years of us
half-learning to do chores
mildewed on top of the special cupboard.
Not the ragbag, where Mom hid bottles
when Grandpa Howe came through town.
And not the stretching place over the oven
where she stashed the Twinkies we couldn't afford.
But down here, skyscraper stacks
of jigsaw boxes, within reach,
almost all midwestern farmhouses, barns and fields,
flowerbeds tripping over themselves to get to the lakes.
Nothing like that around here. 1,000 pieces,
interlocking. Wisconsin, in chunks
all over the table. For weeks
we'd eat standing up,
beans and weiners and instant potatoes
till the last piece fell in
and Mom's eye took on
that thick shine
and we barely breathed, no one even could
step into the room where it lay
finished, settled, clear.
She was saving it for him.

And when he came home
and took one look, mumbling, on the way
to the back bathroom, Mom started it
and we helped,
crumbling in three seconds
the corncribs, the silos, the fields gone
fallow. She'd talk in riddles
for a couple of days.
Nobody understood, but then
we were kids. We never paid much attention.

A *Divorced Mother with Children*

Hanna stands behind a planter box
denting an aluminum pan
on the cranium of her daughter.
The pansies stare,
their pug faces flat,
bewildered as that of Sing Ling,
the crippled neighbor's commie dog
who digs through the vegetable bins,
biting the purple onions of revenge.
Adobe flakes off under the nails
of the sullen girl scratching for balance.
Something breaks inside her mother,
something bigger than tantrums of embroidery,
boil your life down to that
goddammit a turquoise naugahyde
sectional sofa and these kids forever
popping out like varicose
don't lie to me,
shit-for-brains, how many times
I got to tell you—
don't go right from wearing diapers
to changing them.

The Lever Between Her Breasts

Dad slams the door. The floor feels cool.
We cut the feet off my pajamas.
I peek through the hole where the doorknob used to be.
Mom has her glasses off.

Mom makes swiss steak. Dad is late.
We hear the Harley, see the smear of candy-apple red.
He asks everyone out for dinner and another drink.
Mom pours sauce and steak in the trash.

The Watsons break our window with a brick.
Go back to sleep.
Aunt Anna puts our hair in ponytails.
Mom is in a tent because she can't breathe.
Her medicine is all used up.

2.

After the divorce, Mom takes up smoking.
We don't have a box for the poor kids anymore.
Sue watches tv and sucks her thumb.
Ginny learns to fuck and drink. I walk down
drainage ditches. Mom is stark naked
on the roll-away bed. Her makeup's smeared,
her breasts.
I want to stab him, burn him
his pimpled butt leaves me helpless.

3.

Mrs. Palmer insists she is sleeping.
Mrs. Oliver brings chicken and fruit.
Mac touches her fingers till my uncles pry him away.
He was the last, the only name
out of two years of zippers and gin.
In my dream he says, "Breathe. Again. Harder."
She rips the lever between her breasts.
Chest gaping, she heaves that lever through the mirror.
I look at the corpse, but the face keeps changing
into each of us who put her there.

A *Few Chores*

For some moments now I have mourned my organs,
dumped without ceremony in a blue speckled roaster.

  Relatives huddle
  and guess why and why

My daughter, stiff as a charred bird,
fights the gladioli.

  Whistling a tune from a beer commercial,
  a tune he left on my bones—

my body a hand-me-down—he dressed me,
casual as any husband.

  Rubber aprons, bed with a drain.
  My liquids, a pool of blue fire.

Off key, satin sheets, my hair stiff on the pillow.
Won't they see the wire widening the nostrils?

  Burlap sacks and pails of water:
  the assistant dousing blue fire

Such odd labor to deliver an ordinary shell,
the kind you'd notice only if you stepped on it.

Desert Garden

My husband's mother carries a grief
so personal she won't tell even herself.
She expects an extra place to be set.
Her friend she says cut himself on purpose
and pulled back the edges of his wound
to see inside the lives he separated.
A waste, she says.

Looking back, she's a bride again,
slender as a black-and-white aspen
that puts out its first leaves
in a shy trickle like pubic hair.
She comes to her husband
pulling back, not so much
not wanting to share herself
as wanting not to accept a new self inside.

Perhaps we planted too early
or pushed the seeds too far
down the hard rows. Anyway

the few that made it came stumpy,
withered cotyledons drooping,
empty packs clinging to exhausted hikers.

She keeps pulling back till he moves away.
She forgets then to wipe her yellow bee fingers
after swapping dust in the wide
blossoms of crookneck squash.

Mrs. Falbusch

She ran the rooster down herself
and swung the body twice around.
The head in her hand spoke.

The beak's hinge cracked around
its arrowhead of yellow tongue.

She smoothed its comb
and tucked the head
into her breast pocket.

She stood on a chair for her best saucer,
quilted it a cover.

As long as it whispered
she lay awake
confused and aroused like a man.

Baking

His too-short Levi's pinched
at the waist, rounding his hips
to match his fists

fists circling
now over his head
now into his bleached, doughy woman.

The woman, after kneading, begins to rise
becomes puffier, lighter,
trembles as if ready to take flight,
but no, she presses her soft
cheek on the hot sidewalk,

turns swollen
toward her man whining
in the back of the patrol car,
her man, whose face is small.

A Man with a Stocking Cap

A man with a stocking cap
and a walrus mustache
lives inside the peanut.
At night he and his wife
rehash old arguments:
whether to slap
the children or merely
deprive them, who deserves
the first cut
of beef. Their regimen
is the pole they lean from,
the strap that keeps
the golden ring just
out of reach.
The wife's jaw juts
like a brass drawer-pull.

The man goes fishing,
snaps triangles in a can
of corn. He smells
like a used chew, jiggles
Velveeta on his Z-Ray.
Not one mosquito ignores
his torn flannel, his ears.

The Apple

Mother slices
the apple
without sawing,
twirls out
the blossom end,
the seeds with
one crisp swipe. Cross
sectioned womb,
one for me, one
for sister.
Mother with one
hand open
and one fist clenched.

Getting Ready

Each pincurl severe
inside its boundary of scalp
parted off by the rat-tail
anchored with a cross,

you call me in to answer
questions I haven't asked.
You towel your calves,
your soggy breasts

flop like rag dolls
toward your waist
when you stand.
Your tug delivers

the mouse inside you,
nestling in toilet paper
so I won't be afraid
when it happens to me.

The Raisin

A strange cat squats on the far branch
tucked neatly into herself. Our cat hones himself
on his wet sharp words of urge.
I slop a full pitcher to scramble them,
get back in bed still ruffled.
Quiet now, the words get stronger:
their gurgles hiss in my gut.

I mark the liquid snore—
next room, my husband's mother,
whose freak wedge of bone
kept a bullet
out of her sinus, out of her brain.
She dries a little more each day, a raisin,
roasting out that liquid sex no will can cure,
roasting out her leftover life.

Recycling

Disguised as a Cambodian
on a secondhand girl's
bicycle, the messiah
pedals the long way
around the bleachers and parks
between the slow-pitch field
and the dumpsters.
Right away kids
desert the swingsets and slides,
leave the loose tongues
of teetertotters
nagging at the stars.

Weightless, the foreigner
clears the dumpster's lip
in one bound, swallowed up
like an alleycat.
Stands full of mothers
and made-up girlfriends
chop the air
in get-over-here motions
kids pretend not to hear.

Then it begins—
the tinny eruption,
steady molten stream
of Coors, Bud, Schlitz, Oly,
Pepsi, Shasta, Mountain Dew.
A moment of silence.
A glittering shrine.

Ferret-quick
the little man flips
into alley light.
Three times he bows
to his congregation
which has lined up already
a drunken row of dented aluminum.

Not until then does anyone notice
his magical hightop Converse
with stars,
their color of unwashed grapes.

He cups his hands and balances, arms wide.
Celestial wingspan hung with a T-shirt.
Ready with humble muscle,
ready in moth-dusted light,
ready to offer in simple celebration
his ritual of survival.
Missing not one can
the oiled piston of his leg
makes possible a new shape,
a new life, compressed.

Around home the ump and grownups gather
as if it matters
very much to shout
Safe! Out! Safe! Out!

Silent as summer heat
the savior tosses the wafers
clacking into bushel baskets
wired to his back fender.
Quickly as he'd come
he rattles away,
taking refuge in July,
a month that speaks
his language.

Communion

Breaking out of that cloud of forgiveness,
    St. Ignatius, incensed,
paste of Christ still on my tongue,
    I head east. Around one building
rabbits stretch their boomerang back legs,
    fluid in frieze. Outside the Metropolitan
Museum of Art, a steel band
    sets up: pineapples, mangoes, passion fruit
of sound. I opt for the vendor's
    raggedy hot dog, no kraut,
just the infected sauce, red with raw onion.

Then inside, touching the face of a woman
death kept thousands of years ago, this woman
    who painted her eyelids blue
under the same stars I watch row past.
    The guard asks me to take my hand away.
Spine buzzing like the third rail, I marry
    that hand to the sand and wind,
knowing none of us could erase her power.

Calvinism

When the knob on my calf
reached the size of an egg,
my mother held a double-edged blade
in the blue-gas flame.
Look away when I lance it,
she did too, so the putrid spray
hit only her earlobe and the left lens
of her glasses. I misheard her, *abscess,*
and pictured instead, in my leg,
the bottomless hole
sinners fall into, evil ones
cast into my leg, and me
walking around with muscles full
of other folks' deceptions.
No wonder the teakettle screamed,
I did too, as the packs boiled away
layer after layer. My cooled skin
peeled away easily as bologna
once you find the edge.
Remind me to change the wick.
Every day accordian-pleated pressed gauze
tempted the poison out of the wound
until the morning the dressing came away
clean as it went on, and I knew
about limbo, a dance involving a broomstick
and flesh bending back, and I knew about belief,
and the boiling oblivion.